Cute and Cuddly: Baby Animals

FOALS

By Grace Elora

Gareth Stevens
Publishing

Please visit our Web site, www.garethstevens.com. For a free color catalog of all our high-quality books, call toll free 1-800-542-2595 or fax 1-877-542-2596.

Library of Congress Cataloging-in-Publication Data

Elora, Grace.
  Foals / Grace Elora.
    p. cm. — (Cute and cuddly. Baby animals)
  ISBN 978-1-4339-4507-6 (library binding)
  ISBN 978-1-4339-4508-3 (pbk.)
  ISBN 978-1-4339-4509-0 (6-pack)
  1. Foals—Juvenile literature. I. Title.
  SF302.E56 2011
  636.1'07—dc22
                                    2010032882

First Edition

Published in 2011 by
Gareth Stevens Publishing
111 East 14th Street, Suite 349
New York, NY 10003

Copyright © 2011 Gareth Stevens Publishing

Editor: Therese Shea
Designer: Andrea Davison-Bartolotta

Photo credits: Cover, pp. 1, 3, 5, 7, 9, 11, 13, 15, 17, 19, 21, 23, 24 Shutterstock.com

Printed in the United States of America

CPSIA compliance information: Batch #CW11GS: For further information contact Gareth Stevens, New York, New York at 1-800-542-2595.

FOALS

A foal is a baby horse.

5

Most foals are born
at night.

A foal stands up
right away.

Soon the foal runs.

A foal has four hard toes. These are hoofs.

A foal has hair on its neck. This is a mane.

A foal has a tail.
It keeps flies away.

A foal grows baby teeth. It eats grass.

A boy foal is a colt.

21

A girl foal is a filly.

23

Words to Know

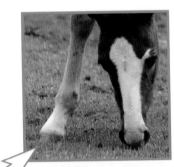
hoof

mane

tail